This be the Answ

Poems from prison

Syed Talha Ahsan

including selections from
"Damascene Portraits" **(2004)**

Radio Ramadan Edinburgh
www.RadioRamadanEdinburgh.com

First published January 2011 by Radio Ramadan Edinburgh

Edinburgh, Scotland.

2nd print February 2011
2nd edition ... 2011
3rd edition 2012

www.RadioRamadanEdinburgh.com

ISBN 978-0-9568106-2-5

Designed and produced by Radio Ramadan Edinburgh
Original Cover Artwork © Zeenath Islam 2011

Contents

Introduction to the 2012 Edition

"They go crazy becuz, Mu, they really believe in the System, and this System always betray those that believe in it! That's what drive them out they minds, man."
  – Delbert Africa, quoted by Mumia Abu Jamal in Jailhouse Lawyers (2009).

"I am a sturdy ship of justice on a sea of overwhelming injustice."
- Talha Ahsan's last words to his family before being extradited to the USA (October 2012).

Syed Talha Ahsan set foot on US soil for the first time on 6 October 2012. He was brought there from England on board a US Department of Justice aircraft. On the same morning – a Saturday - he appeared in the District Court in New Haven, Connecticut charged with various "terrorism" offences connected with his alleged asssociation with an obsolete muhajideen media outlet concerned with Bosnia, Chechnya and Afghanistan. Babar Ahmad, brought to the US with Talha Ahsan, was charged with closely related offences. Three other men extradited with them were arraigned on unrelated "terrorism" charges in New York. All five men have entered "not guilty" pleas.

Talha is being held in solitary confinement and is likely to suffer much more of the same treatment.

The European Court of Human Rights betrayed him. Buckling under political pressure, it decided that Talha's extradition to solitary confinement, along with his co-defendant Babar Ahmad and three other men, would not violate the European Convention on Human Rights. The judgment contradicted the views of many human rights experts, including UN Special Rapporteur on Torture Juan Méndez. It was a disaster for Talha Ahsan and a grave setback for international human rights law.

British courts betrayed him too. The evidence against Talha Ahsan should have been put before a British jury. But the High Court in London refused to grant permission for a judicial review that could have examined British prosecutors' refusal to charge him, and could have looked again at human rights violations in US prisons.

Home Secretary Theresa May treated him as a second-class citizen. Talha suffers from Asperger's Syndrome and a depressive disorder. For him, solitary confinement far from family support violates the international prohibition on cruel and inhuman treatment even more clearly than it does for others. Theresa May could have blocked his extradition for that reason. She didn't.

But ten days after Talha was sent to the USA she blocked the extradition of computer hacker Gary McKinnon – also an Asperger's sufferer – on just that basis. That had clearly been her intention for some time. Her decision to withhold from Talha Ahsan the rights afforded to Gary McKinnon was simply racist. It continues a long tradition of racism in the British and American conduct of the "war on terror" at home and abroad.

Perhaps British and European justice has been subordinated to US political clout. Or perhaps the British authorities have manipulated the US justice system for purposes of their own. For the moment, we can only guess.

Despite the challenges that Talha has to deal with because of his mental health problems, he can still communicate a humanity that can't be found amongst judges, prosecutors and government ministers. It shines out from the poems in this book.

Nearly five times more people are held in US prisons, proportionately to the country's population, than in British prisons. Prisons, and the laws that put people there, ought to matter more to Americans than to Britons. Talha Ahsan's prison poems deserve to find an audience in the USA as well as in Britain.

Richard Haley

Chair www.sacc.org.uk
October 2012

Foreword

Syed Talha Ahsan was arrested at his home in Tooting, South London, on 19 July 2006 by officers from Scotland Yard's extradition unit, pursuant to a provisional warrant under the Extradition Act 2003 alleging offences in America.

He is not some crazed fanatic as portrayed in the media but a quiet, gentle and educated man with a degree from the School of Oriental and African Studies in Arabic.

It is clear from a reading of his poetry that he expresses a passion and commitment to peace.

Playing Devil's Advocate I could say that it is all very well writing a book of poetry now, but he is after all to be indicted in the United States for involvement in international terrorism.

But we should remember Talha is accused in the same case as Babar Ahmad. He has been held since 2006 on a federal indictment from the US state of Connecticut charging him with conspiracy to support terrorists and conspiracy to kill or injure people abroad. The allegations do not relate to domestic terrorism in the UK.

But if they have the evidence why not prosecute him in this country for promoting terrorism abroad? Put him on trial in the UK, he is after all a citizen of this county. I suspect the reason the authorities do not take these steps is that there is no such evidence and that he is another victim of thought crime.

What a tragedy that neither our courts nor our government can offer protection or justice to Talha.

Post 9/11, the US legitimised the detention of so-called "enemy combatants" by presidential order, abolished *habeas corpus* and outsourced torture via rendition to specialist countries, whilst our own intelligence officers stood by and watched.

What kind of justice is it that can see men like Talha extradited to the USA and in the process locked up indefinitely without trial, never permitted to see the evidence against them?

What national emergency is it that allowed Blair to bulldoze these laws through Parliament, other than his bogus war on terror?

Talha Ahsan needs to have evidence presented against him in a UK court and has a right to know why he is in prison.

We need to pressure the government to scrap the Extradition Act 2003, which denies Talha, Babar and others the chance to see or challenge the so-called evidence against them in Britain.

Sending him to a country that tried to legalise torture is not the way forward.

People may find this hard to believe, but under the extradition treaty the government has signed with the US, lawyers are not allowed to challenge any of the claims the US authorities put forward in court.

So in the case of Babar Ahmad, his lawyers could not point out that the tourist map of New York, that supposedly was evidence of plans to blow up the Empire State Building, belonged to his father from his trip to the US in the 1970s!

All that lawyers are allowed to do is challenge extradition to the US on the grounds that human rights will be ignored. The evidence of torture at Guantanamo Bay should leave no one in any doubt that this would be the case.

Such cases are never attractive, if it is a Muslim then human rights are seen as a charter for terrorists. Talha is not asking for much, just justice and the right to be treated as we would want our own brothers and sisters treated. Buy the book, write to him and ask your MP what they will do to get rid of this so-called treaty that abolishes our rights as citizens of the United Kingdom in favour of the US.

Aamer Anwar- Criminal Defence Lawyer

Human Rights campaigner

January 2011

Introduction

Talha Ahsan's poems are little gems. Darts of light leap from them, illuminating the poet's engagement with life, politics and spirituality.

Talha suffers from Asperger's syndrome. He graduated from SOAS, University of London, with first class honours in Arabic. He is now 31 years old and has been in prison in Britain since July 2006. He was arrested at his London home following an extradition request from the United States. But he has never set foot in the United States.

The US indictment against him alleges that he conspired to provide material support for terrorism, provided material support for terrorism, and conspired to kill, kidnap, maim or injure persons or damage property in a foreign country. The charges all arise from Talha Ahsan's alleged participation, while resident in the UK, in the running of what the indictment calls "Azzam Publications and its family of websites." The US District Court in Connecticut which issued the indictment claims jurisdiction solely because one of a number of servers on which the websites were hosted happened to be located in Connecticut.

The indictment covers the period from 1997 to August 2004. The Azzam websites are no longer online, but snapshots of azzam.com, taken at various dates up to about December 2001, are available on the Internet Archive. One of the archived page says that *"Azzam Publications is an independent media organisation providing authentic news and information about Jihad and the Foreign Mujahideen everywhere."* A short document on training for jihad, attributed to Azzam Publications and archived from a related site, says that:

> *"Jihad is therefore an act to liberate people from the oppression of tyrants. Jihad is not illegal acts of terror against innocent people."*

Azzam's choice of material suggests a distinctive viewpoint. It is roughly the viewpoint of the man after whom the website was named. Abdullah Azzam was an Islamic scholar from Palestine who became a key figure in the struggle against the Russian occupation of

Afghanistan. Time magazine called him the "reviver of Jihad in the 20th Century."

This is not a viewpoint likely to find favour with British and US governments. But a viewpoint is not a crime. Numerous liberal intellectuals have promoted invasion and bombing as instruments of humanitarian intervention. Their viewpoint is arguably an incitement to break international law, but it has not led to their prosecution.

Both azzam.com and the US indictment give considerable weight to the struggle for independence in Chechnya. In late 1991 Chechnya declared its independence from the USSR - then on the brink of dissolution - and from the Russian Federation. The Baltic republics of Lithuania, Estonia and Latvia had already declared their independence, as had Armenia and Georgia. All these countries were quickly rewarded with international recognition. Chechnya was not. It nevertheless survived the Russian invasion of 1994-96 and functioned as a *de facto* independent state until its capital Grozny was captured during a fresh Russian assault in February 2000.

The death toll amongst Chechen civilians during the two wars was enormous, perhaps amounting to nearly a fifth of the pre -war population of just over 1 million. Torture, disappearance and murder at the hands of Russian forces were widespread and systemic during and after the war. Abuses continue on a smaller scale to this day. The international community of governments did nothing and continues to do nothing. Many people from the international community of Muslims offered the Chechens whatever practical and political support they could.

The British Government has never branded the Chechen separatist forces as terrorist. No Chechen separatist group has been placed on Britain's list of proscribed organisations. Chechen resistance leader Akhmed Zakayev is based in Britain, where he has been given asylum. Zakayev is the former Deputy Prime Minister of Chechnya and for a time was its Prime Minister in exile. A Russian request for his extradition was rejected by a British court in 2003. The British authorities have made no attempt to bring charges against him, despite the broad terms of Britain's terrorism laws.

If the leader of the Chechen resistance can operate from Britain, how can it be criminal for a British citizen to show support for the Chechen resistance?

The US indictment alleges that Talha Ahsan and Azzam Publications assisted fighters in Chechnya, Afghanistan and elsewhere in ways that went beyond providing sympathetic media coverage. Some or all of these allegations might, if true, amount to offences under British law.

The key evidence against Talha Ahsan comes from computer files seized during a police raid on the home of another London man, Babar Ahmad, in December 2003. So Talha Ahsan is facing charges in Connecticut on evidence obtained by British police from British premises, for offences allegedly committed in Britain. Why? And why have prosecutors in Britain declined to bring charges?

Could it be that the US and British authorities don't like the Azzam viewpoint and want to punish someone - anyone - for it? Might US prosecutors have stretched the evidence to make it point to material support for terrorism and a conspiracy to kill? Might US and British authorities suppose that a US jury would be more likely than a British jury to meet the evidence halfway? Might they suppose that a US court would be less troubled than a British court about the circumstances surrounding the seizure of evidence from Babar Ahmad's house (the Metropolitan Police have admitted to a serious and unprovoked assault on him)?

If that's what they think, they wouldn't just be guessing. The US conviction rate for federal crimes in 2009 was 92%, according to the Department of Justice. The playing field is tilted still more steeply for Talha Ahsan. While awaiting trial he would be likely to be held in solitary confinement under "special administrative measures." Isolation weakens the mind and can leave a prisoner incapable of effective consultation with his lawyer.

If convicted, Talha could receive a life sentence, probably beginning in solitary confinement at the Federal Supermax prison in Florence, Colorado ("ADX Florence"). ADX Florence has been described as a "clean version of hell." Long-term solitary confinement is commonplace throughout the US prison system and afflicts tens of thousands of prisoners.

Long-term isolation is cruel, inhuman and torturous, whatever the reasons for it and whatever the circumstances. Unfortunately, courts in the US and Europe have so far been reluctant to accept that self-evident truth. At the time of writing, the European Court of Human Rights is considering whether, for Talha Ahsan, Babar Ahmad and two others, extradition to the likelihood of solitary confinement would amount to a human rights violation. It has refused to consider any of the other injustices that have been visited upon these men.

Talha has been held for over four years in high -security jails equivalent to an 8-year sentence from a British court. But he has not been charged with any offence in Britain. Nor has any evidence against him been produced in a British court, since the US enjoys a privileged status under the Extradition Act 2003 and is not required to present *prima facie* evidence in support of an extradition request. The decision to prosecute him in the US, coupled with the decision not to prosecute him in Britain, will ensure that his trial is as unfair as prosecutors can make it. Talha Ahsan deserves freedom or a fair trial.

Talha Ahsan's poems are the songs of a caged bird. Read them and enjoy them. But if that is all that you do, you will be a thief. The caged bird's song has this price: that you accept the obligation to do whatever you can to set the bird free.

Richard Haley
Chair of SACC
January 2011
www.sacc.org.uk

Mind the Gap

(   ) until proven (   ),
(   ) and (   ),
anti-(   )

some allegations
the firmer denied
the greater proven,

the chasm between
(   ) and (   ) widens,

jump it,
don't fill it

Wish Harder

perhaps i wished too hard
but a time machine was invented
so i went back in time
where i most wanted
to meet my young mother
when pregnant with me
to trip her up and miscarry me

Untitled

*Houris** still sleep in their pavilions,
Rivers of wine have not passed my lips,
No bough of fruit above my head hangs heavy.

When the doors are locked,
The lights switched off,
It is I who is abandoned in paradise.

*heavenly partner

Return to Exile

The inky waters skim fingers stretched
overboard a boat ferrying me
along on a humid morning:

the chugging has started of throats clearing,
devotees chanting and traders hawking,
competing for attention of multitudes
emerging from verdant banks

Like *jelabis** lifted from boiling vats,
faces crackle at my fumbling vowels.

Only the flitting nightingale with the clipped wings
that day beheld the foreign hum at the door.
She listened with me, as scissors gobbled around
my starving ears, to a song playing on the radio:
my bib could have been its lyric sheet;
the bird's silence a rough translation
and a single tear my understanding.

It's ok, it's unexpected I know.
I am not escaping. I am returning.
* deep fried Indian sweet

Lines for S'ad- *my 'sheikh'*

algerian coffee; the last drop plops,
    utensils clink as this
    unleavened bread-biscuit
    is pushed before me
    never seen before;

this leather bound book not as heavy
in my hands

as in my chest
a brotherly love with parental
    magnitude

that untested mixture
    squishing curiously in my
mouth
    at your insistence

wiping the crumbs' grease
onto the tissue before turning
the page

a foreign sunshine
in a familiar room, in a
settled spot
in front of you

o s'ad! i splutter
"yā walīd! yā `allāma!"
love gasping upon these
foreign words

From *Damascene Portraits*

Lines for *f - the doted on*

fragile hips, angel wings

& a voice rich with sarcasm and wit

i could hear your voice over and over again
until nothing remains but a hiss

eyes nourished by reading

i collected those tall eyelashes from the ground

pious eyelashes!

delicious eyelashes!

i wish i could trap your laughter in a jar - to unscrew and
make me crumble

you refused me, you snubbed me, you mocked
me, you scorned me, & i thought you were so
kind,

disunited by godliness, never united in sin
you're innocent as pollen, you know
you soar about the rest, you're smart, you're
funny

you are what little girls dream to be, you
are the future, you are hope, you're ambition fulfilled
and renewed

you are a name in a book

you are research papers, conferences, you
are what your name is

& somewhere a scrapbook purrs with
its remembrance

Lines for Abu Muhammad- *fellow student*

the waste basket would belch
    fattening upon
this crumpled efforts
and shredded thoughts

    spilling
upon its own weight and
collected uselessness,

"happy people are fatty people,"
    with this love
        unarticulated

these expressions choking the skinny
younger brother, until

obliterated attempts collapse,
he hoping,
as a sufficient obelisk of affection.

From Damascene Portraits

Lines for *h - the failed engagement*

it is not that the

world isn't full of

beautiful things,

    only that some are rare,

like snow,

    that day jebel qaysoun*

shivered with its new expectation

only to melt away,

    frozen as memories and regrets

until one day in the middle of spring

    children run out of school screaming

      pointing to the sky

From *Damascene Portraits*

* *mountain overlooking Damascus*

Private Tuition in Damascus

When peach-soaked mouths unclasp
that is the colour red.

With the toss of spices into the pan,
the muezzins* blitz the city with their calls.

As the last of their summons hisses
into a fading blissful brew,
we simmer into what promise remains.

I'm a seeker and the night is long,
You will teach me worship
is not confined to mosques alone.

*caller to prayer

Paper Clip Chains

He and his mother used to make paper clip chains, with the
Ones covered in coloured plastic lacquer.

She did it because she regarded such things as the most
Ridiculous things in the world.
Did they somehow wish that they would impress their
                                        superiors
Holding together a report four days late?

He did it because he liked the reds, greens, blues and the
Yellows. He liked the feeling of linking one to the other, with
                                        metal
Ends causing bloodless indentations on his finger tips like
Mother's hands.

They would then hold them out, however many- maybe
Fifty, a hundred; she would laugh a while, stop, stagger to
Bed and collapse.

The next morning she would scream at him to undo every
Single one.

Life Sentence

to kill
is to erase an image
off a mirror:

swift glance &
side-step,

no body

just a gaping hole
upon an indifferent world

This be the Answer

A prisoner on his knees
scrubs around a toilet bowl
and the bristles of the brush
scuttles to and fro
as a guard swaggers over
to yell rather than ask -

Where is your God now?

And the prisoner still on his knees
his brush still cleaning answers:

He is with me now, gov.

My God is with me now
hearing and seeing,
whilst your superiors
when they see you, do not look at you
and when they hear you, do not listen to you

My God is risen above the heavens
and closer to me than my jugular vein,

whilst your superiors no different to you
allow you no further than the desk

My God wants me to call Him
whilst your superiors demand you knock

And when I go towards him a hand span,
He comes to me a yard
and when I go to Him walking,
He comes to me running

Ignorance is cured by knowledge
and the key to knowledge is to ask.

Less now the exclamation
and more a question mark,
the guard sulks away,
and a prisoner on his knees,
still, as if in prayer.

Syed Talha Ahsan
HMP Long Lartin, 26th June, 2008

How can I help?

- Contact your local MP to let them know that you are concerned about Talha's treatment in the US
- Send our campaign postcards to the Home Secretary. Contact us for free copies.
- Contribute to the campaign by taking part and making a donation.
- Follow campaign updates on Facebook and Twitter
- Watch 25 minute Extradition Film now ONLINE about Talha Ahsan & Babar Ahmad: www.extraditionfilm.com #ExtraditionFilm

For futher information, please contact:

Free Talha Ahsan Campaign
PO Box 64590
London SW17 8HH
+44(0)7539 659 532

info@freetalha.org
www.freetalha.org
www.facebook.com/pages/FreeTalha-Ahsan
Talha's brother - tweets from family perspective @hamjaahsan
www.twitter.com/freetalha,

For further info:
www.cageprisoners.com/
www.stopisolation.org

solitarywatch.com/
www.friends-extradited.org/